Welcome to Islam

Welcome to Islam

A Step-by-Step Guide for New Muslims

MUSTAFA UMAR

WELCOME TO ISLAM

ISBN-13: 978-1461104773
ISBN-10: 1461104777

www.welcometoislam.co

Printed in the United States of America

In the Name of God
The Most Kind and Merciful

Contents

Introduction

As salāmu 'alaykum [Peace be with you],

Welcome to Islam. Now that you are officially a Muslim, you're probably wondering: ok, now what? So here's some advice on what to do, what to expect, and some other tips for new Muslims.

Each section takes about 10 minutes to read, so try to get through at least one section a day. If you're really motivated, keep reading. You can go through the entire book in about an hour.

Day 1

Welcome to your first day as a Muslim. This is the best decision you have ever made, and I'm sure you thought about it a lot before committing yourself. The first and most important things you should learn are the fundamentals of Islamic belief.

When you accepted Islam, you made this statement: "I declare that there is no other god besides Allah, and I declare that Muhammad is the Messenger of Allah." This is known as the declaration of faith. Perhaps you repeated that statement in the Arabic language as well by saying: "ash-ha-du al-lā ilā-ha ill-all-āh wa ash-ha-du an-na mu-ham-ma-dar ra-sū-lul-lāh".

The moment you *believed* in the truth of that statement, you were already a Muslim. But when you *announced* that declaration publicly, you officially entered into the community of Islam. Now other people know that you are a Muslim and can treat you like their brother or sister in Islam.

The first thing you need to know is what this statement implies. It means that you agree to only worship Allah, the one true God, and never worship anything or anyone else, ever. It also means that you accept Muhammad as being a true Messenger sent by Allah.

The second thing you should do is to memorize that declaration, and repeat it to yourself everyday so that you remember to renew your commitment.

Next, you should know what the words *Islam* and Muslim actually mean. Literally, Islam means "submission to Allah" and *Muslim* refers to "a person who submits to Allah." By entering into Islam, you are submitting yourself to Allah by agreeing to follow the teachings of the Prophet Muhammad as revealed to him.

ISLAMIC BELIEFS

If we had to summarize Islamic beliefs into a few points, we could say there are three:

Unity of Allah

- Allah is the Arabic word for the Creator of everything in this world, i.e. the one true God.

- Islam teaches us that Allah has no partners or equals. That means no one can compare to Him[1] in any way whatsoever. He is superior while everything and everyone else is inferior.

- No one else deserves to be worshipped except Allah, because He is greater than everything.

---

1 The word 'He' does not imply that Allah has a gender. Semitic languages like Arabic don't have a word for 'it', so the masculine 'He' is used as the default. Allah is nothing like His creation.

12

Revelation

- Allah didn't just create us and leave us by ourselves in this world without any guidance. Humans can only figure out certain things in life, so He chose specific righteous people to communicate His message to. By this, we could learn how to live and what to do.

- These chosen people are called Prophets or Messengers. Twenty five of them are mentioned by name in the Qur'an.

- These Messengers were sent to every group of people that ever lived, so there must have been several thousands of them.

- Allah revealed many different books to His chosen Messengers so people could be guided. However, those books were either corrupted or lost over time.

- The last and final book to be revealed was the Qur'an to Prophet Muhammad and is preserved intact and in its original Arabic language.

- The Qur'an was guaranteed to remain intact until the end of time because no other messenger will come after Prophet Muhammad.

Afterlife

- This life is for a limited time only. There will be another existence which will be of infinite length.

- There will be a Day of Judgment where everyone will stand on trial in front of Allah and have to answer for how they lived their life.

- They will be judged by both their beliefs and actions: did they believe in the Messengers that Allah sent and did they live a righteous life as taught by Allah?

- Because life is a test, there will be either the reward of Paradise or the punishment of Hellfire, depending on what people say about Allah and what they do in their lifetimes.

PURIFYING YOURSELF

It is recommended, after you declare your Islam, to go home and take a shower. Entering Islam is like entering a new life. Leave the bad things in your past behind you. When you enter Islam, all of your bad deeds are forgiven. To symbolize that, take a full shower or bath.

INFORMING FRIENDS AND FAMILY

As a new Muslim you must be really excited right now. You might feel like telling everyone you know and love about your acceptance of Islam. This is how Islam spreads, and perhaps your family and friends will also be interested and open their hearts to the message. However, before you do so, my advice is that you should be careful. A lot of people are ignorant about Islam and therefore have a lot of hatred in their hearts. Before you tell people who are very close to you, question them a little bit what they think about Islam and Muslims. For example, you can ask, "Hey Dad, I was reading a book about Islam and found it to be pretty interesting. What do you think?" If you find the answer to be very hostile towards Islam, it might be better to wait to share your news. Quite a few Muslims throughout history, as well as today, have been persecuted by their families and friends after accepting Islam. You have many new things to learn and adjusting to your new lifestyle will be a challenge in itself. So my advice is: if you sense much hostility, keep your Islam a secret , at least for a few months, unless you are financially independent.

WHAT'S NEXT

Thank Allah for guiding you towards Islam and be happy that you have a guidebook of revelation for your life. Remember, take things slow and steady. Don't overload yourself, but don't be lazy either. Keep a balance. May Allah guide you.

Day 2

Welcome to your second day as a Muslim. Now that you know the basic beliefs in Islam, it's time to move on to learning more about the Islamic lifestyle.

CHANGING YOUR NAME

Perhaps you have thought of changing your name, now that you are a Muslim. Or maybe someone else recommended you to do so. Islamically speaking, as long as your name has a good meaning, there is no need to change it. However, if you are named after an idol or your name means something bad, then you must change your name. Some new Muslims prefer to change their name to an Arabic name to signify that they are a new person. However, others prefer to keep their original name, because they are more comfortable with it. It really depends on you: if you feel that your Muslim identity will be strengthened by changing your name, go ahead. You can find a list of names at www.names4muslims.com . Make sure to consult a Muslim scholar before finalizing your decision so you can learn how to correctly pronounce the name.

PRAYER

Islam is a complete way of life. It is much more than just a belief system. Beliefs without action don't have much meaning. We learned about the importance of revelation, that Allah didn't leave us in the dark to figure things out on our own. Could you imagine flying a plane without being taught or having an instruction manual? A human is much more complex than any technological device. So, for a Muslim, the more guidance we get from our Creator, the better off we are. Islam is not a very strict religion, but it does have rules, and these rules are for our own good.

The first requirement on every Muslim, after accepting Islam, is to pray five times a day. There is a certain way to pray and there are specific times. It takes a while to learn this, so just take it slow and steady. Here is what you should learn for today:

WUDŪ'

Before praying, you must wash certain parts of your body so you are in a state of purity before you stand in front of Allah. This is called wudū', or ablution. This is how it's done:

Hands

Go to a sink, turn on the water, and wash both of your hands up to your wrists.

Mouth

Then, cup your right hand and fill it with water. Take that water into your mouth, swirl it around, and then spit it out. Do this three times.

Nose

Then, cup your right hand again, fill it with water, and sniff it into your nose. Be careful not to hurt yourself by sniffing too quickly. Clean the inside of your nose and blow the water out. Do this three times.

Face

Now cup both of your hands and fill them with water. Close your eyes, bring the water to your face, and wash your entire face. Do this three times.

Arms

Now wash your right arm from your fingertips all the way up to the elbow. Do this three times. Now do the same for your left arm three times.

Head

Now, wet both your hands and wipe over your head.

Ears

With the water left on your hands, insert your index fingers into your ears and clean the inside with the index fingers and the back of your ears with the thumbs.

Feet

Lastly, remove your shoes and socks, and put your foot in the sink. Wash your right foot up to the ankle three times. Then wash your left foot three times. You have now completed your wuḍū' and are ready to pray. Seek a knowledgeable Muslim to help teach you in person.

It is not necessary to perform wuḍū' for every prayer. If anything comes out of your private parts [like urine, excrement, or gas] or if you go to sleep, you must renew your wuḍū' again.

If you have intercourse, or even a wet dream, you must shower and wash your entire body in order to get into a state of purity for prayer.

Menstruating women should not perform the five daily prayers during their period. The same applies to women during their post-natal bleeding period after giving birth. This is a mercy from God because of their condition and they don't even need to make up the prayers later. However, they should remember God in their heart throughout the day and continue to learn more about Islam.

TIMINGS

The five prayers are spread throughout the day, so you are always remembering Allah. To make life easy for us, Allah has given a span of time in which we can offer our prayers conveniently. Each prayer takes about 5-10 minutes and each span of time is usually an hour or more . Prayer timings depend on the position of the sun,[2] so they change every day and vary from place to place. To find out the prayer times in your area, go to www.islamicfinder.com. Type in your zipcode and click 'go'. On the right column of the page, you will see a table that looks like the one below:

Today's Prayer Time	
Day	Thursday
Fajr	5:21
Sunrise	6:29
Dhuhr	12:07
Asr	3:19
Maghrib	5:45
Isha	6:54

Let's go over this table as an example. The first prayer of the day is called Fajr and begins at 5:21AM. This prayer ends at sunrise which is at 6:29AM. This means you can pray the Fajr prayer anytime between these two times. The second prayer of the day is Dhuhr, and begins

---

2   This used to be the way people determined time before watches were invented.

at 12:07PM. This prayer ends before the next one starts at 3:19PM. So you can pray the Dhuhr prayer anytime between 12:07PM and 3:19PM. The third prayer of the day is Asr, which is between 3:19PM and 5:45PM. The fourth prayer, Maghrib, begins at sunset, which is at 5:45PM and lasts until 6:54PM. The final prayer is Isha and begins at 6:54PM and lasts until 5:21AM of the next day, just before Fajr. Try to memorize the names of these prayers if you can because they are used by all Muslims. It is strongly recommended that you pray each prayer as early as possible and not delay unnecessarily. Being lazy in observing prayer on time reflects your attitude towards God. Try to never miss a single prayer. In case you do, make it up, with a feeling of regret, as soon as you are able to do so, even if the time has passed.

DIRECTION OF PRAYER

Prayer can be performed anywhere: in a park, a shopping center, a parking lot, etc. When praying, all Muslims in the world face toward the direction of the city of Makkah in Arabia. This unites all Muslims around the world. To find out the direction, go to www.qiblalocator.com and type in your zip code. A red line will show you which direction you should face. Either figure out the direction through the map or use a compass to determine the location. This will be the direction you always face, so you only need to check once for each location. This direction is called the 'qiblah' in Arabic and you should calculate it for your home, school, or work.

22

FIVE TIMES A DAY

As mentioned before, prayer takes some time to learn, so take it slow and steady. After you have made wudū' and determined the direction of prayer, sit down for a few minutes during one of the prayer times and just thank Allah for guiding you to Islam. Until you learn more, this will be your prayer. Do it five times a day to get used to the prayer timings and used to performing wudū'.

WHAT'S NEXT

Remember, take things slow and steady. You will eventually get used to the prayer and it will get easier to wake up early if you sleep a little earlier. Don't overburden yourself, but don't be lazy either. Keep a balance. May Allah guide you.

Day 3

Welcome to your third day as a Muslim. Now that you know a little about prayer, you've begun to learn the first duty to your Lord. Today, we will learn more about prayer. Remember, it takes time to get used to, so take it slow and steady.

PRAYER MOTIONS

Now that you know how to prepare for prayer, you are ready to learn the motions and what to say, so you can follow the way that Prophet Muhammad taught us to pray. Prayer should be done in Arabic, because that is the original language of the Qur'an. Don't worry; you don't need to learn a whole new language. You can just memorize some Arabic phrases that you need in order to perform the prayer and learn what they mean.

Prayer takes some time to learn. No one is expected to learn the entire prayer in one day. This book will only show you the motions and a little of what to say. If you can visit a mosque or have other Muslim friends to pray with, you will be able to pray with them. Just follow them in the number of times that they perform the motions and you will learn the rest eventually. There is a person who will stand in front and lead the prayer and everyone else behind him will follow.

Throughout the prayer, you will be standing, bowing, sitting, and prostrating. Each position has a physical posture as well as a spiritual meaning. Focus on how to perform these stances and learn a few Arabic phrases for now.

THE PRAYER MOTIONS AND STANCES

Read the description of each position, look at the picture, and try to practice doing it yourself. Ask another practicing Muslim to help you if needed.

Standing

Front   Side

Stand facing towards Makkah. Keep your hands to your sides. Your feet should be about shoulder width apart.

Your eyes should be focused[3] on the ground a few feet in front of you.

This is the stance of a person at full attention who is focused.

Raising Hands

Front   Side

Begin the prayer by raising your hands near your ears. Make sure your palms are facing forward.

This signifies that you are leaving all other thoughts in your mind behind as you begin connecting with God.

---

3   Remember, during the prayer, you may close your eyes for concentration whenever you want.

Standing for Recitation

Front   Side

Use your right hand to grab your left hand at the wrist. Place both hands on your body above your navel.

This is a stance of humility which shows your awe and respect in front of God.

Bowing

Front   Side

Bend down and grab your knees. Keep your fingers slightly spread apart. Your eyes should be focused where your feet are. Try to keep your back straight as much as possible.

27

This is a stance of humbling the body before God by lowering it in a bowing position. It reminds us of our place in front of God.

Prostration

Slowly get down on your knees. Place your hands on the ground in front of you. Put your forehead and nose on the ground between your hands. Keep your hands flat on the ground near your ears with your fingers together and facing forward. Make sure your elbows are off the ground. You should be standing on your toes with the rest of your feet off the ground.

Front   Side

This is a stance of the utmost humility where you put your face, which represents your honor, on the floor in front of God.

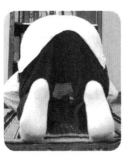

Back (Feet)   Side (Feet)

Sitting

Sit on the floor with your hands on your thighs near the knees. Keep your fingers together. If you are able to, sit on your left foot while standing on the toes of your right foot which is a little out to the side. If this position is difficult, sit in any comfortable way.

Front

Side

This is supposed to be a comfortable and relaxing position which gives you a break after having stood for a while.

Back (Feet)

Side (Pointing)

Finish the Prayer

Right Salam   Left Salam

Conclude the prayer by moving your head to the right while looking over your right shoulder. Then move your head to the left in the same way.

While moving your head right and left, you will also learn to say a greeting of peace. It means that you are praying for all the people around you.

WHAT TO SAY DURING PRAYER

We will now learn what to say during the prayer. These are the Arabic phrases that we will use:

ARABIC	ENGLISH
al-lā-hu ak-bar	*God is the greatest*
sa-mi-al lā-hu li-man ḥa-mi-dah	*God has heard the one who praised Him*
as-salāmu 'alaykum wa raḥmatullah	*May the peace and mercy of God be with you*
al-ham-du lil-lāh	*Praise is due to God*

You will notice that, when praying in a group, the leader of the prayer will say the first three Arabic statements out loud. Look at the meanings and try to memorize them if possible. If possible, have someone experienced help you pronounce them. Don't worry about pronouncing them perfectly for now. That will come with time.

There are a lot more Arabic phrases which are said throughout the prayer. However, whoever doesn't know them or forgets, they are supposed to praise God by saying: 'al-ham-du lil-lāh'. During prayer, whenever the prayer leader is quiet, keep saying 'al-ham-du lil-lāh' quietly to yourself throughout the prayer.

PERFORMING THE PRAYERS: STEP-BY-STEP

Prayer consists of a number of units, or cycles, where you repeat much of what you do and say in each unit. There are three different types: a two-unit, three-unit, and four-unit prayer. The five daily prayers consist of all three types, so you will need to learn all of them eventually. However, for now, try to pray in a group as much as possible.

Remember, it is better to seek a knowledgeable Muslim or an instructional book to help teach you the motions and how to say the Arabic statements. There is more to prayer which you will eventually learn, but this is a good start for now.

WHAT'S NEXT

Try to memorize some of the Arabic statements. If you can't, then at least memorize the English translation and say it in your prayers for now. Try to attend as many prayers as possible inside the mosque or with a group of Muslims. May Allah guide you.

Day 4

Welcome to your fourth day as a Muslim. Now that you know how to pray when you are in a group, you've begun to fulfill the first obligation in Islam. Today, we will learn some things which are prohibited in Islam for a Muslim to do. Remember, these prohibitions are for your own good and will make you a better person. It may take some getting-used-to, but it's not that hard.

DRESS CODE

Islam is a religion of modesty and purity. It not only focuses on creating a better individual but a better and purer society. To facilitate this, it has certain guidelines on how a Muslim should dress in public and behave in front of the opposite gender.[4] There is no specific style or color of clothing in Islam. Fashion changes depending on time and place. What people used to wear 50 years ago in one place is radically different today. Islam is open to change, as long as it is bound by certain moral principles. Therefore, the dress code in Islam consists of certain general principles

---

4   See Qur'an 24:30-31, 17:32

only. Anything that fits the principles is fine to wear. Since men and women are naturally different in their physical makeup, the guidelines for dress are different.

Men

When in public, men are required to cover from their navel to their knees, at minimum. This means that they should not walk around in their underwear or in extremely revealing shorts.

Women

Women are required to cover their entire body in public with the exception of their face, hands, and feet. To do this, a woman will usually wear any type of loose fitting clothing like a long skirt and a top and then cover her hair and neck with a headscarf. To get an idea of what to wear, visit www.shukronline.com. Muslim women dress modestly to prevent inappropriate glances and behavior. Tight and revealing clothing usually sends the opposite message.

Dress for Prayer

The guidelines for dress in public also apply for prayer, even if you are alone. This is done out of respect, the way you wear nice clothes when going to meet important people. So when praying, make sure to cover what must be covered, out of respect for Allah.

DIET

Islam is a relatively easy religion. Almost everything that Allah created on Earth as food can be consumed. There are just a few things which we aren't allowed to eat or drink. More than 99% of all different types of food is lawful, or Halāl, while less than 1% is unlawful, or Harām.

Swine and its Byproducts[5]

A Muslim is not allowed to eat pork, ham, bacon, sausage, pepperoni, gelatin, or anything else containing pig. The pig is a very unclean animal, so Allah has prohibited eating any part of it. Make sure to check the ingredients of certain foods that may contain parts from a pig like bacon bits in clam chowder or gelatin in jello . It only takes a few seconds to look for it and there are so many non-pork alternatives available, you won't miss a thing.

Alcohol & Drugs[6]

Anything that can intoxicate a person is prohibited in Islam because you lose your intellect and can't think straight. Allah is so concerned with this illness in society that he has prohibited taking even one sip of alcohol or one puff of a drug although it can't intoxicate you. This is because many people may lose control at some point and end up getting drunk or high. So make sure to avoid beer, wine, marijuana, or any other drug that alters your mind. Don't even go near them. If you are addicted, you may need to enroll yourself in a rehabilitation program. Quitting might take some time, but Islam will help you build the discipline you need to get clean.

---

5   See Qur'an 2:173
6   See Qur'an 2:219, 4:43, 5:93-94

Dead Animals[7]

Humans are omnivores. We eat both plants and animals. However, when it comes to animals, there are some restrictions because animals are living beings. Most people eat beef, chicken, goat, and lamb, which are all permissible in Islam, with one requirement: they must be slaughtered in a specific way so that the blood drains out of the animal and it is sacrificed in the name of Allah. This type of slaughter is performed by Muslims and is called Halāl or Ẓabīhah. A Muslim should only eat meat that has been slaughtered in this way. Go to www.zabihah.com to find out where you can find this meat in your area. All seafood can be eaten without these requirements.

ECONOMICS

There are some financial rules that Islam has put into place in order for a better society to function. Not only does it prevent immorality in individuals but it leads to a more cooperative society.

GAMBLING[8]

A Muslim is not allowed to gamble or bet in any way, shape, or form. Whether the odds are against you or in your favor, it is an illegitimate way to make money. Gambling is an illness and a disease, and Islam puts a stop to it before it can ruin a family or society, the same way even one sip of alcohol is prohibited.

---

7   See Qur'an 6:121
8   See Qur'an 2:219

INTEREST

Charging interest on money that is lent out leads to immorality and injustice in a society. Therefore it is prohibited in Islam, whether the amount is large or small. In order to minimize the effects of interest, Islam has also prohibited paying interest on loans. If you are already in debt, try to get out of it as soon as possible. If you have accounts which are collecting interest, change them to checking accounts which have the least amount of interest given, and give that amount of interest you earn in charity. If you have a mortgage on your house, ask your local Muslim scholar what to do. Islam teaches us to live within our means and buy what we can afford. A Muslim will always pay their credit card bills on time to make sure no interest ever has to be paid.

WHAT'S NEXT

Try to adjust your lifestyle as much as possible. It may be a little difficult at first but you will feel great once you get used to it. Don't overburden yourself, but don't be lazy either. Keep a balance. May Allah guide you.

DAY 5

Welcome to your fifth day as a Muslim. Now that you know most of the basics of Islam, you will have to prepare for the journey ahead. There is a lot to learn and do, and it will come with time. Today, we will learn about staying connected with Muslims through the Friday prayer, the sources of Islam, and some advice about challenges that new Muslims might face.

FRIDAY PRAYER

It is obvious that you will not be able to make it to the mosque for all five prayers every day. However, it is important to go as much as possible to meet other Muslims and stay in contact with them. This is why Islam has set a special prayer on Friday afternoon, when all Muslims are required to attend the mosque, listen to a motivating sermon, pray, and meet other Muslims. All adult Muslim men must take time off from their work and attend this prayer if there is a mosque nearby. Women and young children are excused if they are busy, but they should try to attend at least sometimes. It is unfortunate that Friday is not a holiday, but you have a legal right to take off an hour or more for religious reasons as long as you make that time up.

THE SOURCES OF ISLAM

Everything that you have learned so far about Islam has been derived from the two sources of Islam: the Qur'an and the Sunnah.

The Qur'an is the direct revelation from Allah to the Prophet Muhammad. It is the guidebook that Allah has given us to follow and the only revealed book from the Creator that has been authentically preserved, without change, addition, or deletion.

The Sunnah refers to the teachings, wisdom, and way of life of the Prophet Muhammad. His statements and actions are compiled by scholars in books, and each one is called a Hadīth. These Hadīth have different levels of authenticity; some are weak and some are strong, so you must be careful about what to follow. In time, you will learn to tell the difference. Ask your local Muslim scholar in the meantime.

These two sources, the Qur'an and the Sunnah, determine what Islam is and isn't. If you see a particular group of Muslims doing something and you want to determine whether what they are doing is from Islam, something cultural, or something against Islam, just check to see if it is in the Qur'an or the Sunnah. You do not always need to go directly to the sources themselves. Reading different books about Islam can be easier because they will focus on one topic and explain things in a manner that is easier for the average person to understand.

COMMON CHALLENGES

Remember, life is a test, so there will naturally be some challenges along the way. Here's a heads up on some of the most common challenges that new Muslims will face:

Information Overload

There is a lot to learn in Islam and sometimes you might feel overwhelmed with so much information coming your way. You may meet Muslims or read some more advanced books that assume you know more than you actually do. Take things slow and steady. Learning is a gradual process. Don't get overwhelmed and try to keep a steady pace in your study of Islam.

Lack of Discipline

Islam presents a balanced way of life and is never over burdensome. In the beginning, it can take a while to get used to some things and quit some bad habits. Try to take your new religion seriously and commit yourself. Allah will help you along the way, so you never need to feel as if you aren't strong enough to do it yourself.

Being a Part of the Community

Don't isolate yourself from the greater Muslim community. Make new Muslim friends, regularly visit the mosque, and get involved with the community. The people you hang around with define who you are. There is nothing wrong with having non-Muslim friends, as long as they are not a bad influence on you. However, try to spend more time with your practicing Muslim friends who can have a very positive influence on you.

Persecution

Throughout history, believers have been persecuted for their faith. It is something which Allah tests people with, in order to see whether they are dedicated. Perhaps you may not face any persecution whatsoever by friends, family, or coworkers, but if you do, remember that Allah is with you and that the Muslim community is there to help. Do not hesitate to ask your brothers and sisters in Islam for assistance. If your civil rights are being violated, contact www.cair.com.

Finding the Balance

You will meet many different Muslims and come across several different books on Islam. One of the things that may initially confuse you is when you see a Muslim saying something about Islam and then another Muslim saying the exact opposite. Which one of them is correct? In order to figure things out, you should consult a Muslim scholar. There is no class of priests by birthright who define what Islam is. A Muslim scholar is someone who has studied Islam in depth and has a deep knowledge of the Qur'an and the Sunnah. These scholars will be able to tell you what has a basis in Islam and what has been made up. Scholars will also disagree with each other sometimes over minor issues, but that is because Islam allows room for different scholarly opinions in things such as where to place your hands when praying. Be careful of websites made by random people about Islam and books written by unqualified or ignorant Muslims. Check the credentials of the author in case you feel uneasy about something they are saying.

WHAT'S NEXT

Now that you know the basics of Islam, try to practice as much as possible. Be sincere in your faith. Know that you will make some mistakes along the way, but keep moving forward. Get a book or video teaching you the details of prayer. Attend as many lectures, events, and seminars as you can about Islam. Most importantly, read the Qur'an on a daily basis, even if it is just one verse.

Glossary of Arabic Phrases

Here are some common Arabic phrases that Muslims use:

- When greeting another Muslim, we say: as-sa-lā-mu a-lay-kum—*"Peace be with you"*

- When responding to that greeting, we say: wa a-lay-kum as-sa-lām—*"And peace be with you"*

- When intending to do something in the future, we say: in shā al-lāh—*"If God allows"*

- When appreciating something, we say: mā shā al-lah—*"God did what He willed"*

- When thanking someone, we say: ja-zā-kum-ul-lā-hu khay-rā—*"May God reward you"*

- When happy about something, we say: al-ham-du lil-lāh—*"God be praised"*

Recommended Sources

WEBSITES

http://www.welcometoislam.co

http://www.quran.com

http://www.whyislam.org

http://islamtoday.com

http://qa.sunnipath.com

http://www.islamqa.com

ISLAMIC ITEMS

http://www.islamicbookstore.com

http://www.soundvision.com

VIDEOS

http://www.thedeenshow.com

http://www.halaltube.com

Made in the USA
Lexington, KY
06 July 2014